LIVING WITH OBESITY

ABDO
Publishing Company

LIVING WITH OBESITY

by L. E. Carmichael

Content Consultant
Amanda S. Bruce, Assistant Professor, Department of
Psychology, University of Missouri–Kansas City

LIVING WITH HEALTH CHALLENGES

CREDITS

Published by ABDO Publishing Company, PO Box 398166, Minneapolis, MN 55439. Copyright © 2014 by Abdo Consulting Group, Inc. International copyrights reserved in all countries. No part of this book may be reproduced in any form without written permission from the publisher. The Essential Library™ is a trademark and logo of ABDO Publishing Company.

Printed in the United States of America,
North Mankato, Minnesota
092013
012014

 THIS BOOK CONTAINS AT LEAST 10% RECYCLED MATERIALS.

Editor: Melissa York
Series Designer: Becky Daum

Photo credits: Maryna Kulchytska/Shutterstock Images, cover, 3; iStockphoto/Thinkstock, 8, 16, 18, 30, 36, 39, 42, 46, 53, 56, 70, 75, 85, 96; Shutterstock Images, 14, 92; Roswell Daily Record, Andrew Poertner/AP Images, 22; BananaStock/Thinkstock, 24, 50; Comstock/Thinkstock, 26; Eyecandy Images/Thinkstock, 34; Fuse/Thinkstock, 60; Shelby Allison/Shutterstock Images, 64; Wavebreak Media/Thinkstock, 66, 88; Stockbyte/Thinkstock, 78; Alilia Medical Images/Shutterstock Images, 83

Library of Congress Control Number: 2013945897

Cataloging-in-Publication Data

Carmichael, L. E.
 Living with obesity / L. E. Carmichael.
   p. cm. -- (Living with health challenges)
Includes bibliographical references and index.
ISBN 978-1-62403-246-2
1. Obesity--Juvenile literature.   I. Title.
616.3--dc23

2013945897

CONTENTS

EXPERT ADVICE

I am a licensed clinical psychologist and a university professor. Though I study and teach about obesity and eating, even I struggle at times to eat healthy foods and exercise! I also have three young children whom I hope will grow up to make healthy decisions as well.

While I'm at work, I spend a lot of my time conducting research about how the brain is involved in food motivation, eating behaviors, and obesity. Scientific studies show that physiologically, we as human beings are "wired" to like calorically dense foods. We naturally are drawn more to donuts than to lettuce. Unfortunately, calorically dense foods are often the unhealthiest foods.

We live in a sedentary culture (we have to go out of our way to exercise!) that is also saturated with calorically dense foods. Fast-food restaurants are everywhere. And advertising constantly encourages unhealthy eating. Because of this, we are fighting both our brains and our environment when we make healthy choices in eating and exercise. Making good choices is not easy, but it is not impossible either. Here is some advice to keep in mind:

It is important to remember that you are not alone. Find a support system that will encourage you to make healthy choices. This could include friends, parents, aunts, teachers, uncles, grandparents, or counselors.

Eating and exercise are both important. If you cut down on unhealthy foods and eat more fruits and vegetables, that's awesome! But don't forget to do some physical activity, too! Walking and climbing stairs are simple ways to help improve your fitness.

Be wary of advertising. We are bombarded with messages about how to eat, where to eat, and what to eat. Yet the vast majority of these foods are not good for us. Do your best to be a critical consumer, and be skeptical of what you see and hear.

Every single small healthy decision you make helps. Walking for ten minutes is better than not walking at all. Taking the stairs instead of the elevator is great! Eating an apple instead of a brownie for a snack is an excellent choice.

Remember that a series of small healthy decisions can lead to positive habits and outstanding lifestyle choices.

—*Amanda S. Bruce, Assistant Professor, Department of Psychology, University of Missouri–Kansas City*

THE SKINNY ON FAT: DEFINING OBESITY

Ashley went to the party to see Tyler. No, that's not true. She went to watch Tyler. "Seeing" Tyler implied he might actually see her back, and despite the dozen classes they'd taken together since ninth grade, she was pretty sure that had never happened.

Being overweight can sometimes make you feel as though you are invisible.

As far as the stars of the varsity hockey team were concerned, heavy girls were invisible. And invisible was how she felt, lurking in the corner by the snacks until she finally gave up and caught the last bus home. She didn't know why she kept putting herself through this—it's not as though anything ever changed.

Ashley knew she wouldn't be able to sleep unless she calmed down. A hot shower was just what she needed. She covered the bathroom mirror with a towel and started to undress. Her jeans had left a deep, angry, red divot around her middle, and she had to wiggle to get them down over her thighs. She cracked the window to let the steam out and climbed into the shower.

There was a breeze, and when she climbed back out, the towel covering the mirror had fallen to the floor. For the first time in more than a year, Ashley stared at her reflection, unable to believe what she was seeing. That swollen, puffy face couldn't possibly be hers. But it had to be. The eyes looked the way she felt inside—trapped.

Heart racing, Ashley fumbled under the vanity for her mother's bathroom scale. She stepped on and waited for the numbers to stabilize: 204 pounds. *204 pounds*. "How did this happen?" she wondered.

GLOBAL OBESITY STATISTICS

The numbers are undeniable: weight is a problem around the globe. Worldwide, obesity has almost doubled since 1980.[4] In 1997, the World Health Organization declared obesity a global epidemic. Sixty-five percent of people on Earth live in countries where obesity causes more deaths than malnutrition.[5] At 79 percent, the Pacific Island of Nauru has the highest prevalence of obesity in the world.[6]

OBESITY: A GLOBAL EPIDEMIC

If you're like Ashley, you may have been gaining weight for years without realizing how much. Or maybe you've noticed your pant size is increasing, but you deliberately avoid thinking about it. Or worse, your doctor, parents, or peers might have called you obese. If so, you are not alone.

In the United States, the prevalence of childhood obesity is rising steadily, and as of 2012, almost 32 percent of American kids and teens were overweight or obese.[1] One in five European children is overweight.[2] In 2010, the International Obesity Task Force estimated that 200 million school kids are affected worldwide.[3]

These statistics are alarming, for reasons that have nothing to do with appearance. Obesity is a major risk factor for a number of serious physical health conditions. In the United

States, obesity is the second leading cause of preventable death, surpassed only by smoking.

As Ashley put it, how did this happen? The causes of the global obesity epidemic—also called globesity—are complex, but there is a simple explanation for why individuals gain weight. It's called energy imbalance.

FOOD, ENERGY, AND WEIGHT

To survive, you have to eat. Food provides raw materials for manufacturing muscle, bone, and DNA. Food also contains nutrients your body can't make for itself. And food has energy that powers cell and body functions.

Food energy is measured in calories. The number of calories you spend on breathing, pumping blood, and maintaining body temperature is your basal metabolic rate (BMR). You burn additional calories whenever you move, whether you're texting or playing basketball.

Eating more calories than you need for fuel creates an energy imbalance, and your body stockpiles the excess. First, your muscles and liver fill up with glycogen, enough for one day's BMR. Your body converts any additional calories to fat molecules and stores them in your adipose tissue.

Adipose tissue provides cushioning for your bones and organs and contributes to growth, metabolism, brain function, and temperature insulation. It's made up of fat cells, cells that specialize in energy storage. Each cell contains a fat globule that grows when fat is stored and shrinks when you access that hoarded energy. If you consistently store more food energy than your body can use, you gain weight.

DEFINING OBESITY

Obesity is defined as an unhealthy excess of body fat. It's measured by calculating body mass index (BMI):

$$\text{kilograms of weight} \div (\text{meters of height})^2$$

DIGESTION AND ENERGY

Understanding digestion and energy can help you understand and control your weight. Your stomach holds approximately eight cups (2 L). Digestion breaks food into small molecules your body can absorb. Most nutrient absorption occurs in your small intestine, which is 20 feet (6 m) long. Because the inner surface of your small intestine is wrinkled, its surface area is equal to that of a baseball diamond.

A calorie is the amount of energy needed to raise the temperature of one-fifth teaspoon (1 ml) of water 1.8 degrees Fahrenheit (1°C). There are 1,000 calories in every Calorie (kilocalorie) listed on a food label. The average BMRs for adults are 1,300 to 1,500 calories for women and 1,600 to 1,800 calories for men. These BMRs are approximately the same amount of energy required to run a 100-watt lightbulb for one day. One pound (0.45 kg) of body fat equals about 3,500 calories.

Adults are overweight if their BMI is 25 or higher. A BMI greater than 30 is considered obese.

Measuring obesity in young people is more complicated because healthy levels of body fat change during growth. After calculating your BMI, your doctor compares it to the range of BMIs in kids of the same age and gender. If your BMI exceeds that of 85 percent of teens of your age and gender, you're overweight. A BMI greater than 95 percent of comparable teens means you're obese.[7]

CALCULATING BMI

Not sure if your weight is healthy? Visit http://apps. nccd.cdc.gov/dnpabmi/ and enter your date of birth, date of measurement, sex, height, and weight. The calculator will determine your BMI and compare it to kids of the same age and gender.

For example, a ten-year-old boy who's five feet (1.5 m) tall and weighs 110 pounds (50 kg) has a BMI of 21.5. That's higher than the BMIs of 93 percent of ten-year-olds, making this boy overweight. A 13-year-old boy with the same height and weight also has a BMI of 21.5, and it's higher than only 81 percent of boys his age. The 13-year-old is therefore in the healthy weight range for now.[8]

If you become obese at a young age, your risk of developing health complications is higher than if you gain weight as an adult. This is a frightening reality, but understanding the causes

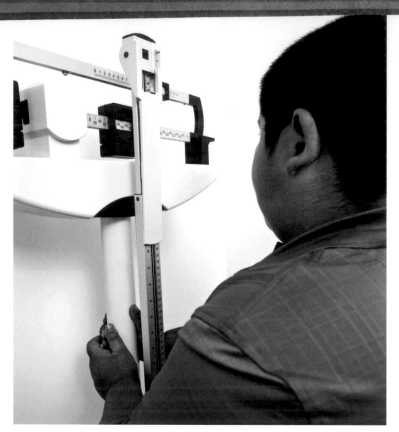

A BMI measurement compares your weight to your height.

and effects of obesity will give you the tools and motivation you need to take control of your health—today and for the future.

ASK YOURSELF THIS

- *Do you avoid scales, mirrors, or other indicators of your weight?*

- *Has someone told you you're overweight or obese? How did those labels make you feel about yourself?*

- *What factors might be contributing to obesity around the globe? Are any of these factors at work in your life?*

- *Occasionally, everyone eats for reasons other than hunger. Has eating for celebration, comfort, stress, or boredom become a habit for you?*

- *Are you worried your weight might be affecting your health? What would you be willing to do to get or stay healthy?*

THE LIMITATIONS OF BMI

BMI is calculated using total body weight, which includes muscle and bone, not just fat mass. As a result, athletes and weight lifters might have high BMIs even though they're perfectly healthy. To more accurately predict health risks associated with obesity, doctors estimate body fat using several additional methods. Doctors measure skinfold thickness to determine how much fat is under the skin. With bioelectrical impedance, doctors determine body composition from the speed at which electricity passes through the body. And dual X-ray absorptiometry scans give a direct measurement of body fat, muscle, and bone.

GANGING UP: NATURE, NURTURE, AND YOU

Zach plugged some change into the school vending machine and pulled out a soda. It was a hot day, and he wanted something to drink while he waited for his dad to pick him up. When Zach was in junior high, his family had lived in the suburbs and he had walked

Pizza and fast food are convenient but can contribute to weight gain.

home every day. But his family had moved, and there weren't any sidewalks between the high school and their new apartment. He didn't mind, though. Pops worked two jobs, and the 20-minute car ride was about all the time they got to spend together.

"Your Ma's got the chance for some overtime tonight," Pops said when he finally pulled up to the curb. "Pizza or burgers?"

"Pizza," Zach said right away. He was tired of burgers, but pizza gave him endless options. And tomato sauce counts as a vegetable, right? Zach missed home-cooked meals, but the economy was bad, and both his parents were working twice as much as they used to just to survive. He worried about the effect all the work was having on their health—and not just his parents' health. Ma said full figures ran in the family, but they had all gained a lot of weight lately.

Pops dropped Zach at home and rushed away to his evening shift. The air was starting to cool outside, and Zach wished he could meet some friends at the basketball court down the street. But the hoop was long gone, and the court was gang central. They were in the midst of another turf war, so Zach's parents had made him swear not to leave the apartment after dark.

A tendency toward obesity can run in families.

Instead, he grabbed the pizza and another soda and headed to his computer. He sighed. It was going to be another long, lonely night.

OBESITY: IT'S IN YOUR GENES

Weight gain results from energy imbalance, but it's not quite as simple as eating too much or exercising too little. Dr. Jack Shonkoff, director of Harvard's Center on the Developing Child, explained,

> *Both nature, by which we mean genes, and nurture, meaning experience, affect each other. And they're inextricably intertwined. Is there a genetic predisposition to obesity? Absolutely. Is obesity caused by an environment and behavior? Absolutely.*[1]

Very few of these complex, interacting factors are fully under your control.

If you're like Zach, obesity runs in the family. By 2004, researchers had identified more than 200 genes involved in metabolism, food consumption, energy use, and other weight-regulating functions. Scientists disagree about the total impact of these genes on obesity, but there's no doubt your DNA matters: identical twins, whose DNA is also identical, often have comparable BMIs even when they grow up in different family environments.

One gene linked to youth obesity is *MC4R*, which is mutated in 4 to 6 percent of children with severe obesity.[2] *MC4R* causes food-seeking behavior from the age of six months, overeating, and increased fat storage, among other symptoms. Another gene is *Ob*, which codes

NEVER SATISFIED: PRADER-WILLI SYNDROME

Most cases of obesity have multiple causes, but some result from mutations in single genes. One genetic mutation, Prader-Willi Syndrome, causes obsession with food, insatiable hunger, and learning disabilities or other mental disabilities. Prader-Willi affects one in 10,000 to 25,000 children, and because patients never feel full, they have a very high risk of developing obesity.[3]

To cope with Prader-Willi syndrome, families use games, puzzles, and physical activity to divert attention from food and create routines that regulate when meals occur and what's eaten. Some families lock up food to relieve the emotional stress kids feel because they want to eat but know they shouldn't.

INDIVIDUAL OR ENVIRONMENT?

Your risk of obesity is higher if you meet one or more of these criteria:

- **You're female**
- **You're Native American, a Hispanic boy, or an African-American girl**
- **You're Caucasian and from a low-income family**
- **Your parents are not well educated**

The reasons for these differences aren't fully understood, but they probably originate with living environment. For example, supermarkets are associated with healthy diets including fruits and vegetables, but African-American and Hispanic neighborhoods have 50 and 70 percent fewer supermarkets, respectively, than predominantly Caucasian neighborhoods.[5]

for the hormone leptin. Leptin was discovered in obese mice in 1994 and is linked to early-onset obesity in children. Another gene linked to obesity is *FTO*, which a Dutch study showed to be mutated in 88 percent of overweight kids.[4] The *FTO* mutation causes people to choose large volumes of energy-dense foods, which can lead to obesity.

THE OBESOGENIC ENVIRONMENT

Global obesity is worsening so quickly many scientists place the blame on changing lifestyles rather than genes. Australian researcher Boyd Swinburn called "the sum of influences that the surroundings, opportunities, or conditions of life have on promoting obesity in individuals or populations" the obesogenic environment.[6] The easy availability and low cost of energy-dense foods—such as Zach's soda and pizza—are aspects of this environment.

In the 1960s, the average dinner plate was nine inches (23 cm) wide. Today, it's 12 inches (30 cm).[7] Fast-food restaurants are also notorious for supersizing, which increases portion size while lowering cost. Maximizing food value in this way can be a priority, especially for families in Zach's situation.

Unfortunately, foods that cost less are usually high in energy and low in nutrition. The average American eats one pound (0.45 kg) of sweeteners, flour, processed fat, French fries, and high-fat dairy products every day.[8] French fries and potato chips account for one-fourth of all vegetables eaten in the United States.[9] These foods may taste great, but they significantly increase your risk of obesity.

PLUGGED IN: SCREEN TIME AND OBESITY

Spending a lot of time in front of a computer or television can dramatically affect your weight. People eat 14 percent more when distracted by television.[10] Teens with televisions in their bedrooms are 31 percent more likely to be overweight than teens without.[11] Including all media, average screen time for kids ages 8 to 18 is 7.5 hours per day.[12] Cutting back on watching television leads to significant reductions in BMI. The American Academy of Pediatrics recommends young people spend less than two hours per day using televisions, DVDs, video games, and computers.

Recognizable characters such as Ronald McDonald or characters from popular cartoons help market food to children.

As access to calories has increased, opportunities for physical activity have declined. Only 2 percent of American high schools require daily physical education, and fewer kids are participating in after school sports.[13] If you live in a neighborhood similar to Zach's, you may not have access to green spaces, fitness facilities, or other environments permitting safe exercise.

The importance of environment can't be overlooked. It's so tightly linked to obesity risk that geography is a better predictor of weight than age, ethnicity, or socioeconomic status. For example, young people living in new suburban areas are 34 percent less likely to be overweight than those in rural and urban neighborhoods.[14]

YOUR BRAIN IS WORKING AGAINST YOU

Despite abundant scientific evidence to the contrary, many people still believe obesity results from bad choices. But how much control do you really have over your own decisions?

Human behavior is strongly influenced by reinforcement—punishments or rewards that follow a particular choice. Because food is necessary for survival, it's a powerful positive reinforcer. The reward value of a particular food is affected by taste, variety, availability,

ADVERTISING WORKS . . . AGAINST YOU

New research suggests that although television viewing is a sedentary behavior and conducive to obesity, advertising may be a bigger risk factor for obesity. Advertising is big business. In the United States, food and beverage companies spend $10 billion annually on marketing to children.[15] The average child sees 5,500 food commercials a year.[16] Most foods advertised during peak television viewing times—91 percent—are high in sugar, fat, or salt.[17]

Food logos cause your brain to activate centers involved in motivation and reward, similar to the way your brain responds to actual food. This activation is stronger in kids who are obese. In one study, preschool kids claimed food in branded packages tasted better than identical food wrapped in generic packaging.

A Canadian study showed that kids who watch American television eat significantly more cereal than French-speaking kids who watch channels programmed in Quebec. Quebecois channels banned marketing to children in 1980.

It can be difficult to break the cycle if your brain associates food with rewards from an early age.

advertising, and energy density. Because parents often promise sugary or high-fat treats in exchange for good behavior, kids begin associating food with rewards from an early age.

Because of the way the brain develops during childhood and adolescence, teens anticipate rewards more strongly than adults do. Young brains also react more powerfully upon receiving rewards, encouraging youth to take risks, including choosing unhealthy foods high in fat, sugar, salt, or a combination of the three.

However, the reward value of specific foods changes the more you encounter them. Initially, the intensity of your brain's response encourages you to overeat. With repeated exposure, your brain reacts less strongly, causing you to eat a larger volume of food to achieve the same sense of satisfaction you experienced previously. This creates a vicious cycle of obesity that can be extremely difficult to overcome.

ASK YOURSELF THIS

- *Does obesity run in your family? How might this affect your ability to achieve a healthy weight?*

- *What aspects of your family's lifestyle might be affecting your health?*

- *How easy is it for you to purchase healthy foods where you live?*

- *What sedentary activities, such as watching television or playing video games, could you replace with physical activity?*

- *Have you noticed that a food you love just doesn't taste as good anymore? What does that suggest about your brain's response to it?*

OBESITY IS BAD FOR YOUR HEALTH

D ylan tugged his laces and then
straightened up, barely able to hide
his grin. His teammates jostled and
cracked jokes while the newbies shuffled
nervously around them. Dylan sympathized. He
remembered what it was like last year, when he

Dylan's weight became a problem when he found he could no longer do his favorite activities.

was still waiting for his shot. But now, he was part of the football team—at least he would be if Coach ever showed up to start the tryouts.

On cue, Coach Randall strode onto the field, fiddling with his clipboard. He scanned the line of boys, and his eyes caught Dylan's. "Whoa, Tank! Looks like you put on a few since last season." Dylan shrugged. Yeah, he hadn't trained in months, and he'd gone up a pant size or two, but it's not like his weight was a problem—it's what made him such a good linebacker.

Coach assigned them laps to get a sense of how they could move. Dylan took off around the track. At first, everything felt solid, but soon his feet started hurting. He figured his shoes must be worn out. He'd hit the mall that weekend and look for a new pair. Dylan pushed past the pain, but then something else started happening. He was only on the second lap, but his heart was going like he'd run miles. It was like his chest wouldn't expand—his breath was coming in great, wheezing gasps.

Dylan staggered to the edge of the track and slumped over, bracing himself on his aching knees. "What's wrong, Tank?" Coach asked, but Dylan couldn't get enough air to reply. He sank to the turf as Coach whipped out his cell phone and dialed 911. He could see it in his teammates' faces—if Dylan couldn't run laps, how could he run defense? He realized he wasn't going to make the team.

If you're like Dylan, your weight may be compromising your ability to participate in activities you love. It's also possible that basic life tasks, such as mowing the lawn or climbing stairs, have become too challenging to complete comfortably. If so, you may be experiencing health conditions caused by obesity. The higher your BMI, the greater your risk of developing health complications.

FIGHTING FOR BREATH

Scientists estimate 15 to 38 percent of asthma cases in adults are caused by obesity.[1] The link between weight, wheezing, and asthma is less clear in young people, but in one recent study, kids with BMIs above the 85th percentile were 61 percent more likely to wheeze than kids with lower BMIs.[2]

Obstructive sleep apnea, which prevents normal breathing during sleep, affects 30 to 50 percent of obese teens.[3] The condition contributes to snoring, daytime sleepiness, poor school performance, hyperactivity, and aggression in kids, and it increases the risk of heart disease in adults. Scientists aren't sure how obesity generates breathing problems, but weight loss significantly improves these conditions.

ADULT-ONSET DIABETES

Because of obesity, kids and teens are now developing health conditions that used to occur only in adults. In most obese youth, the first such condition is insulin resistance, a precursor of type 2 diabetes mellitus (T2D). T2D, commonly referred to as adult-onset diabetes, isn't just an adult disease. It now occurs in kids—some as young as eight years old.

Insulin is a hormone that moves glucose out of your blood and into your cells, where it's used for energy. If you're obese, your body needs more insulin to do this job than a

WEIGHING DOWN THE BONES

Body weight exerts downward pressure on leg bones. In rare cases, the pressure causes them to permanently bow, a condition called Blount's disease. Studies show obese kids also have less bone mass than kids with lower body weights, perhaps due to the poor nutrition and low activity that often contribute to their condition. Improper bone growth is irreversible and can lead to painful complications later in life, such as arthritis.

Pain can also be an immediate consequence of excess body weight, which places additional physical strain on the body—imagine climbing a flight of stairs versus doing so with a stack of textbooks. Up to 39 percent of obese teens experience pain in their backs, feet, or knees.[4] This discomfort can perpetuate obesity, as you're less likely to want to exercise if you already hurt or it causes you pain.

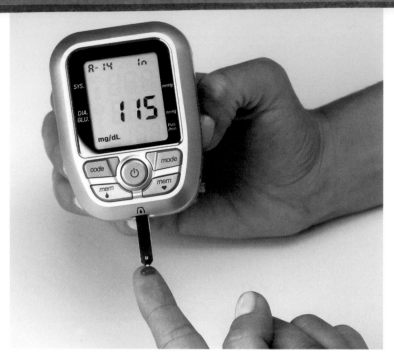

Type 2 diabetes is one complication associated with obesity.

body with less stored fat. At the same time, an obese body loses its ability to respond to insulin and becomes resistant to the hormone. As blood-sugar levels increase, your pancreas produces more insulin but is unable to keep up with the demand. Eventually, high blood sugar destroys the insulin-producing cells, leading to T2D.

One in three North American kids will probably be diagnosed with T2D in their lifetimes. Your risk depends on several factors, including BMI, age, location of fat, race, and family history:

- For every 2.2 pounds (1 kg) gained, the prevalence of diabetes increases by 9 percent.[5]

- The younger you are when you start gaining excess weight, the higher your risk.

- Visceral fat is more dangerous than subcutaneous fat.

- African-American, Hispanic, Pima Indian, and Asian kids tend to be more insulin resistant than Caucasian kids with the same BMI.

- If your relatives have T2D, you are more likely to get it.

The early stages of insulin resistance don't have symptoms. Four percent of kids have no idea they have T2D until their blood sugar spikes so high it causes a coma.[6] These comas

LOCATION, LOCATION, LOCATION

When it comes to stored body fat, location is everything. Visceral fat is much more dangerous than subcutaneous fat. High levels of visceral fat increase your risk of asthma, diabetes, heart disease, and cancer. In fact, teens with a high ratio of visceral to subcutaneous fat have a greater risk of weight-related diseases than teens with higher BMIs but lower ratios.

To estimate how much visceral fat you have, your doctor will calculate your waist-to-hip ratio. In adult men and women, a ratio below 0.9 or 0.7, respectively, is generally considered healthy. You can get a quick idea of your ratio by looking in the mirror. A pear-shaped body is less likely to develop health complications than an apple-shaped body.

are sometimes fatal, so if you're at risk for T2D don't wait: talk to a doctor today.

RISKING A BROKEN HEART—AND MORE

In adults, insulin resistance is the first stage of metabolic syndrome, a major risk factor for heart disease and stroke. Metabolic syndrome affects 25 percent of adult Americans.[7] There's no agreed-upon definition for metabolic syndrome in young people, but many obese teens experience some or all of the symptoms experienced by adults:

- Hyperlipidemia—high levels of fats in the blood, especially LDL (low-density lipoprotein), or "bad" cholesterol. In one study, obese youth had nine times more LDL cholesterol than kids with healthy weights.[8]

- Atherosclerosis—fat deposits on the inner walls of blood vessels that partially block blood flow. These plaques begin forming in children as young as nine.

- High blood pressure—increased force exerted by blood within the arteries. Obese kids ages five to 18 are nine times more likely to have elevated blood pressure.[9]

- Increased ventricular mass—thickening of the muscular walls of the heart's lower chambers, caused by the extra strength required to pump blood around a larger body.

Any one of these conditions increases your odds of heart disease or stroke, but risk factors seldom occur alone. A study of 49,220 kids in 23 countries showed elevated BMI increases the likelihood you'll have multiple risk factors, raising your overall risk.[10] Early detection is important, so ask your doctor to test for indicators of metabolic syndrome.

OBESITY CAUSES CANCER

According to the American Cancer Society, 51 percent of new cancers in women and 14 percent of new cancers in men are linked to obesity.[12] Twenty percent of deaths from cancer in women are related to obesity.[13]

Obesity increases the risk of cancer of the breast, colon, esophagus, gallbladder, kidney, and pancreas. Some evidence suggests risk of blood cancers such as leukemia may also increase. Scientists don't yet understand why obesity increases cancer risk, but changes in hormones, including insulin, are probably involved.

CHILDHOOD OBESITY PREDICTS ADULT OBESITY

It's very unlikely you'll experience a heart attack or stroke while still a teenager. But if you're an obese teen, you have up to an 85 percent chance of becoming an obese adult.[11] Risk factors for obesity-related diseases may follow you into adulthood, with potentially deadly consequences. A 2011 study by the National

A high percentage of obese teens remain obese as adults. The younger you are when you become obese, the greater your chance of future complications.

Institutes of Health predicted that, as obese adolescents age over the next 25 years, the rate of adult heart disease will increase from 5 to 16 percent.[14]

In the United States, approximately 112,000 people die each year from complications of obesity.[15] Worldwide, that number may be as high as 2.8 million.[16] Adolescent obesity is a better predictor of early mortality than adult obesity. Because of this, many experts believe your generation will have more illnesses and shorter life spans than your parents'—the first time in modern history the trend of increasing life spans is expected to reverse.

ASK YOURSELF THIS

- *Have you given up favorite activities or dreams because of your weight?*

- *Do you often have muscle or joint pain without an obvious cause?*

- *Do you have a family history of diabetes or heart disease, which could increase your own risk?*

- *Are you an apple or a pear in shape?*

- *Do you wake up choking, feel tired in the morning, or have other symptoms that might be caused by sleep apnea?*

- *If your weight stays the same or increases as you age, how might it affect your life?*

SHRINKING LIFE SPANS

Years of life is the difference between the life span of a healthy-weight person and an obese person. Studies show an obese individual will lose between five and 20 years of life compared to a healthy-weight 20-year-old of the same race and gender.[17] Age, BMI, and weight-related diseases also affect years of life lost. For example, a ten-year-old with T2D will lose 19 years.[18] An 18-year-old with a BMI greater than 25 has a significantly higher chance of dying before age 38.[19] While these trends are true on average, it's worth noting 20 percent of people with a BMI greater than 40 live healthy, full-length lives.[20]

THE UGLY TRUTH ABOUT WEIGHT STIGMA

Hannah sat down at the back of the locker room, legs quivering. She hated the fitness tests Ms. Rosen made them do every month. No matter how much Hannah had improved, the physical education teacher seemed convinced she wasn't trying. Someone

Weight stigma makes some people dislike PE or stop trying hard in the class, which in turn reduces the amount they exercise and contributes to weight gain.

needed to tell Rosen shouting wouldn't increase motivation.

With her gym shirt hanging like a shield around her neck, Hannah found the sleeves of her sweater and pulled it over her head. In the moment she was blinded by fabric, there was a burst of giggling from the end of the row. At least it wasn't about her this time. The other girls were chattering about the senior trip: the class was spending a day at the water park. Hannah wasn't going. The looks and whispers she got during the swim unit were bad enough—there was no way she'd "celebrate" in a bathing suit.

By the time she got home, Hannah was starving. Her mom was unloading groceries, and Hannah snagged a bag of chips. Mom grabbed her wrist. "Eat the carrots instead," she said, "or we'll have to get your prom dress altered again."

Glaring, Hannah took the tub of dip to dunk her chips as well. She was sick of hearing it all day at school, and she really didn't want to get it at home, too.

The salty, greasy snack helped her mood until she suddenly realized she'd finished the entire bag. Hannah's anger rushed back, but now she was mad at herself. No one would ever see past her size if she couldn't stop eating! Hannah ran for the bathroom, desperate to purge the calories. She would be thin like her mother, Rosen, and the girls at school. She promised herself she'd skip breakfast for a month if that's what it would take.

ORIGINS AND SOURCES OF WEIGHT BIAS

Weight prejudice has pervaded Western culture since the 1800s. Advertising, entertainment, and value systems reinforce these discriminatory beliefs, and they've become widespread. Researchers estimate that weight discrimination has increased by 66 percent over the last decade and is now as common—and as inexcusable—as racism.[1]

MEDIA AND MARKETING

Weight stigma in popular culture goes beyond the casting of underweight actresses. Shows such as *The Biggest Loser* and *Bulging Brides* send a clear message: it's acceptable to humiliate the obese. Research shows the more television boys watch, the more likely they are to negatively stereotype overweight females, and watching just one episode of *The Biggest Loser* significantly increases weight bias in the viewer.

Media coverage of Britney Spears's personal struggles including her weight gain and weight loss from 2007 to 2009 epitomizes society's tendency to equate body size with character. A more recent example is retailer Abercrombie & Fitch's refusal to carry large sizes because they market to "the attractive, all-American kid with a great attitude and a lot of friends."[2]

Many people who are overweight or obese have felt others' bias against them.

Stigma resulting from weight bias is often the first negative consequence of teen obesity. For many, negative social effects are harder to endure than any medical complications arising from their condition.

In 1967, researcher Robert Staffieri showed six- to ten-year-old boys drawings of three body types: thin, muscular, and obese. Boys called the muscular figure strong, popular, brave, and good looking. When describing the personality of the obese figure, they chose words such as lazy, dirty, stupid, ugly, liar, and cheat.

Children display bias against obese peers by the time they're three years old. This prejudice intensifies with age and is stronger among kids who believe people's weight is

THE ECONOMICS OF WEIGHT BIAS

If you're female, weight stigma can have long-term effects on your education, employment, and social success. Obese women are less likely to be accepted to college, despite excellent qualifications, and less likely to receive financial support from their families to pay for education. They are less likely to be hired, promoted, or paid the same wage as women with lower weights, and they are more likely to be living below the poverty line.

controlled by choices rather than medical conditions. Girls are even biased against healthy weights, showing a preference for BMIs doctors define as underweight.

If you're an obese teen, you've probably experienced prejudice from adult sources, too. One-fifth of middle- and high-school teachers believe obese teens are untidy, emotional, and less likely to succeed, setting lower expectations for them as a result.[3] In 1999, 14-year-old Gina Score died at a boot camp program because counselors denied her medical care after a run, believing she was faking her fatal heat stroke.

Some doctors, dietitians, and other professionals who treat obesity are also biased against those who have it. If you've encountered this, don't let it prevent you from seeking the medical care you deserve—find a new doctor instead.

In surveys, 34 percent of overweight boys and 47 percent of overweight girls have said their families nag or tease them about their weight, and these experiences are some of the most painful.[4] One 75-year-old obese woman shared her experience:

> My father was always telling me I was fat because I was lazy. I have always been active, but I didn't participate in athletics in school. I was in marching band, chorus, and other more academic pursuits, so, therefore, I was "lazy." To this day, I feel guilty if I sit down to read a book or magazine.[5]

BULLYING AND ITS CONSEQUENCES

Bullying includes physical violence, teasing, humiliation, shunning, and spreading rumors, and it can happen in person or online. Obese teens are more likely to be targets than almost

OBESITY ACROSS CULTURES

The weight stigma typical of Western Caucasian cultures is not universal. African-American women are less likely than white women to experience stigma. In Polynesian cultures, a large body is desirable because it signifies power, wealth, and beauty. Obesity is so positively perceived in Gambia that many people deliberately attempt to gain weight. As in most cultures, however, attitudes toward weight are strongly sex-biased. As of 2006, 32.6 percent of Gambian women older than 35 were obese, but less than 2 percent of men were.[6]

If you feel bullied, speak up and ask an adult you trust for help. You do not deserve to be bullied because of your weight.

any other group, and the higher your BMI, the higher your risk. In the highest BMI brackets, 63 percent of girls and 58 percent of boys experience bullying.[7]

Bullying can distract you at school or tempt you to skip class, affecting your grades as a result. Overweight teens in Thailand have significantly lower GPAs, and in the United States, obese teens who've been teased are 50 percent less likely to succeed academically in school.[8] Weight-based bullying is so stressful it often raises the victim's blood pressure, affecting physical health.

Ninety-four percent of overweight kids believe the teasing they receive is unfair.[9] At the same time, however, 91 percent feel ashamed of their weight, suggesting a sense of personal responsibility for their condition.[10] Have you become convinced obesity is your fault or that you deserve to be bullied? This is called internalization of stigma and it has serious consequences for your mental health and your emotional health. Obese teens who internalize are more at risk for psychological complications than those with higher BMIs who don't internalize. The complications can be painful—even deadly. They include poor body image and

WHEN YOU NEED TO TALK

Coping with weight stigma is difficult, but you don't have to do it alone. If you need support, start with your family. Studies show that strong family relationships protect against the impact of weight bias. If your family is a source of stigma, ask someone you trust to support you while you tell them how it makes you feel. In addition, a doctor, psychologist, counselor, or social worker can help you manage the complications of weight bias.

If you or someone you know is suicidal, act immediately. Talk to a trusted adult or call a suicide hotline. Visit www.suicidehotlines. com for a number in your area.

low self-esteem, anxiety disorders, depression, risk-taking behaviors, and suicide.

Unhealthy body image develops very early. By age seven or eight, boys in Staffieri's study wanted to look like the muscular figure. For girls, the chance that body image will affect self-esteem is even higher.

Obesity sufferers experience anxiety and depression more often. These mental illnesses are three to four times more common in obese people than in the general population.[11]

Risk-taking behaviors affect obese teens more than their healthy-weight counterparts. Obese teens are more likely to smoke or drink, to self-mutilate, and to develop eating disorders such as unhealthy dieting, binging, vomiting, or use of diet pills.

Finally, obese teens who are bullied are two to three times more likely to consider suicide than those who aren't.[12] The perception of being overweight—even if untrue—is a stronger predictor of suicide risk than high BMI alone.

Your weight does not give others the right to abuse you. Tell a parent or responsible adult what you're experiencing, and the next time you're victimized, stay calm, stand up straight, and look your bully in the eye. For more tips for dealing with bullies, visit www.pacerteensagainstbullying.org.

ASK YOURSELF THIS

- *Do you make assumptions about your own or someone else's character, intelligence, or lifestyle based solely on weight?*

- *Have you noticed subtle forms of weight bias, such as narrow public seating or stores that don't carry large sizes?*

- *If you or someone you know is being bullied, how can you help?*

- *How can you let your family know that teasing, even if it's well-meaning, is actually destructive?*

- *Are there ways you can help others recognize the serious consequences of weight bias?*

QUALITY OF LIFE

Quality of life can be affected by school success, social relationships, and education and income levels. Physical and mental health make a big difference, including life limitations due to physical or emotional challenges, physical abilities, and pain, all of which affect your energy and zest for life.

Obese kids and teens report a quality of life comparable to that of kids with cancer. This is surprising, because cancer requires lengthy and aggressive medical treatments that obesity doesn't. This finding may indicate the serious impact of weight stigma.

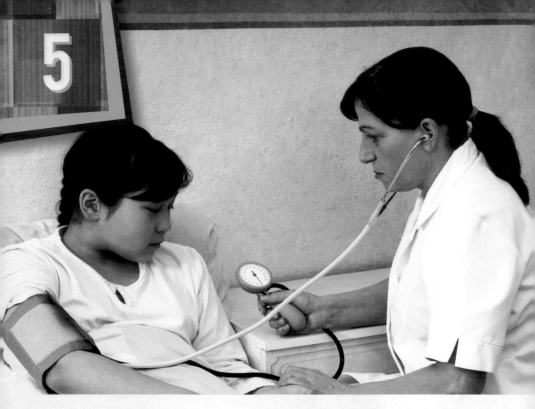

AN OUNCE OF PREVENTION, A POUND OF CURE

L exi beat her heels against the side of the exam table, waiting for Dr. Haddad. It had been a week since her mom first dragged her to the clinic. Lexi held out as long as she could, but Mom had watched some obesity show on television and wouldn't let it go. To get things back to normal, Lexi finally agreed to the weighing, the blood pressure cuff, and the horrible paper gown. But all that wasn't as bad as the blood tests—the real reason Lexi avoided doctors. She hated needles.

Mom shifted in her chair, twisting the strap of her purse between her hands. She had been a wreck ever since the nurse called to book this follow-up appointment, but Lexi wasn't worried. She felt fine, so there couldn't be anything serious wrong with her.

At last, Dr. Haddad entered. His expression was grave. Mom sat up straight. "Alexis, I'm sorry to have to tell you this," he said, "but you have type 2 diabetes." Mom grasped for Lexi's hand, tears welling in her eyes, but Lexi was too stunned to respond. She couldn't be sick. She felt fine.

Dr. Haddad continued talking, something about "lifestyle changes" and "medication" and, worst of all, "regular blood tests," but Lexi was having trouble understanding. Did this mean she had to stop eating chocolate? Would she have to spend hours in the gym? Worse yet, would she have to stick herself with needles *every single day*?

Lexi wished she were six years old again. She would eat more veggies and run around

THE FOUR STAGES OF TREATMENT

The American Medical Association recommends four stages in the treatment of adolescent obesity:

- **Stage 1—Your family doctor supervises dietary, activity, and behavioral changes.**
- **Stage 2—If your health does not improve after three to six months, dieticians and counselors may join your health-care team.**
- **Stage 3—Your team will help you set specific lifestyle goals with a built-in system of rewards.**
- **Stage 4—Specialists may recommend very-low-calorie diets, drug therapy, or bariatric surgery to accompany your lifestyle changes.**

outside and never gain a single extra pound. That way, none of this would have ever happened.

STOPPING OBESITY BEFORE IT STARTS

Lexi's wish to go back in time to prevent obesity is a good one. Many experts believe prevention is the best treatment for obesity, and it has to start early—even before birth! That means parental health and education will be pivotal to reversing the obesity epidemic, for several reasons.

If your mother was obese or undernourished during pregnancy, your risk of obesity increases. Maternal health affects a fetus's epigenetics— the control and regulation of genes involved in obesity. These genetic "memories" may or may not be reversible later in life.

Breast-feeding plays a role, too. Breast-fed babies can control their own energy intake. Formula feeding can lead to overeating because parents encourage babies to finish the bottle.

How you ate growing up is a factor, too. If your parents told you to "clean your plate" as a child, you probably overate. But if they did the opposite, restricting your food options, your body might have overcompensated by stockpiling available energy.

The types of food you ate also have an effect. Research in mice shows early exposure to high-fat and high-sugar foods alters how the brain responds to these rewards, which can make you more vulnerable to obesogenic environments. Avoiding these foods during childhood reduces their reward value later on.

Another reason prevention is vital is that each fat cell can store only so much energy. If your body needs more space, it produces

HEALTHY SCHOOLS, HEALTHY TEENS

In 2007, the US Department of Agriculture found 94 percent of school lunch programs failed to meet federal health standards.[1] Since schools are also reducing opportunities for physical activity, most teens spend the bulk of each day in obesogenic environments.

Studies show school health education leads to significant reductions in students' BMIs. The Centers for Disease Control has resources to make schools healthier. But don't feel like you have to wait for the adults to take action. In 2011, a nine-year-old in the Philippines started his own campaign to ban soft drinks from schools.

If you are told to clear your plate as a child,
it might contribute to later obesity.

extra cells. You generally make these cells
during three stages of life: before birth, between
ages three and seven, and during puberty and
adolescence.

Once fat cells are created, they will change size, but they will never go away. This makes significant weight loss extremely challenging.

Prevention will protect your own children someday, but if you're like Lexi, it might be too late to work for you. If you believe you are overweight and are concerned about potential health complications, it's time to make a doctor's appointment.

PREPARING FOR YOUR APPOINTMENT

Your doctor will ask you about your lifestyle, so it will help to be prepared. In the days leading up to your appointment, keep a journal of food intake, physical activity, and sedentary pastimes. This might be surprising or uncomfortable, but be honest and record everything. The details you provide will help your doctor develop a targeted plan. Also, be sure you're familiar with your family's health

THE PROTECTIVE EFFECT OF GOOD SLEEP

Sleep influences the hormones that control hunger and cravings, meaning if you're sleep deprived, you're at increased risk of obesity. The average teenager needs approximately nine hours each night. Improve your sleep with these simple tips:

- Stop drinking liquid after 8:00 p.m.
- Avoid caffeine in the six hours before bedtime.
- Relax before bed by avoiding stressful activities for at least two hours.
- Remove television and game systems from your bedroom.

history—a family tendency toward diabetes or heart disease can increase any risk resulting from your weight.

Your doctor will weigh and measure you to calculate your BMI. You can also expect skinfold measurements or other tests to check your ratio of visceral to subcutaneous fat. If your doctor doesn't order blood tests, ask about them even if you hate needles. Checking hormone, cholesterol, and blood-sugar levels will help your doctor determine whether you've developed any weight-related diseases. Insulin resistance is usually the first health issue to affect teens, and treating it early can prevent you from developing other more serious physical complications.

THE REST OF YOUR LIFE

A diagnosis of obesity will change your life. Don't panic—the alterations might not be as dramatic as you imagine or fear. If you're still growing and your BMI is near the 85th percentile for your age and gender, your doctor will probably recommend working to maintain your current weight. That way, your BMI will decrease naturally as you get taller.

If your BMI is above the 95th percentile or you've passed your final growth spurt, you've got a longer road ahead of you. Weight loss will be necessary to reduce your risk of disease, and it requires adjustments to your diet and activity

Even small lifestyle changes and slight weight loss can improve your health and quality of life.

levels you'll need to maintain for the rest of your life. This prospect can be intimidating, but it's important to recognize even small decreases in weight can dramatically improve your health. Instead of thinking about what you might have to give up, focus on the health and physical freedom you're going to regain.

FOR BETTER HEALTH, JUST SAY 5-2-1-0!

The Childhood Obesity Foundation suggests four simple ways to radically improve your health. Remember 5-2-1-0:

- **Kids who eat five (5) or more servings of fruit and vegetables per day are significantly less likely to become obese than those who eat fewer than three.**
- **Kids who clock more than two (2) hours of daily screen time are twice as likely to be overweight than kids logging less than one. Get that television out of your bedroom!**
- **Moderately strenuous physical activity for just one (1) hour per day is all it takes to improve your health. This includes walking, biking, and household chores. You're more likely to stick with it, though, if you pick something you enjoy.**
- **Cut sugar-sweetened beverages down to zero (0). A 13-year-old boy must jog for 50 minutes to burn the 260 calories in a 20-ounce (590 ml) bottle of soda, and one can per day increases your risk of obesity by 60 percent.[2]**

ASK YOURSELF THIS

- *Do you view health or appearance as a stronger motivator for weight loss?*

- *Are you prepared to change your lifestyle to improve your health or quality of life?*

- *Do you plan to have children someday? What would you be willing to do to protect them from obesity?*

- *Have you ever used a food journal? Did the record surprise you?*

- *Is your school environment obesogenic? What could you do to improve it?*

HEALTHY EATING FOR A HEALTHIER YOU

I t had been almost a year since Anna blew out her knee trying to land a double axel. She'd never minded being the heaviest girl in her figure skating class, but when her doctor said she couldn't try jumps again until she got her weight to a healthier level, she knew she had to do something. She loved skating too much to quit.

The first few months were brutal. Anna tried every crash diet she found on the Internet, plus a few her friends suggested. They all worked, at least for a week or two. But sooner or later, the cravings took over, she'd snap and pig out, and the pounds would pile on worse than before. She got so desperate she even used her emergency credit card to order a bottle of fat-burning supplements from a late-night infomercial. Anna stopped taking them, though, because they made her heart race and feel weird.

As she was flushing the rest of the fat-burning pills, Anna realized it was time for a new strategy. Instead of changing her entire diet at once, she decided to make one small modification at a time. Soda and energy drinks were the first things to go. Downing nothing but water was tough at first, but she lost three pounds in three weeks, and that made it easier to keep going. After a while, taking the next little step toward healthier eating started to feel like a game—one she might be able to win.

Anna stopped losing weight as fast as she did initially, but her knee hadn't hurt lately, either. She was going for a checkup with her

THE STATS ON SUPPLEMENTS

Losing weight is difficult, so it's understandable 34 percent of people have tried diet supplements.[1] Unlike prescription medications, however, over-the-counter pills and powders are not regulated by the US Food and Drug Administration. There's also very little scientific evidence to suggest they actually work. In addition, supplements can interact with medications your doctor has prescribed and have side effects ranging from diarrhea to anxiety, trouble sleeping, and heart problems.

Never start a supplement without checking with your doctor first. And if it sounds too good to be true, it probably is!

doctor soon. With luck, he'd give her permission to jump again. Landing that axel would make up for every calorie she had to cut.

TAKING IT SLOW

If you've just committed to improving your health through weight loss, you probably feel like Anna did at first. You want to slim down as quickly as possible. When it comes to conquering obesity, however, speed is counterproductive. As hard as it can be to take it slow, plan to lose no more than one to two pounds (0.5 to 0.9 kg) per week if you want to keep them off.

Changing your diet is the fastest way to lose weight. However, dieting—making extensive, temporary changes to your eating habits—doesn't work in the long term. As Anna did, focus on changes you're going to be able to live with.

COUNTING CALORIES

Low fat, low carb, high protein—variations in dieting advice are confusing and endless. No matter how they're marketed, every trendy diet is based on the same principle—energy deficit. Eating fewer calories than your body needs forces it to burn stored energy. In other words, you lose weight by reversing the energy imbalance that caused the gain.

Creating an energy deficit is not about going hungry. It's about getting the most food for your caloric buck. In studies, people eat the same volume of food, regardless of energy density. Foods that contain lots of water or air—such

THE DANGERS OF DIETING

Going on a diet is not the same as healthful eating. Dieting—an extreme, temporary change in eating behavior—is a risk factor for a range of eating disorders, and it can actually stimulate weight gain. For young people, dieting has additional risks. Kids who restrict caloric intake because they fear obesity may not enter puberty, and extreme undernutrition in childhood increases risk of breast cancer later in life.

In contrast to dieting, healthy eating involves reasonable portions with a good balance of nutrients. If you need to lose weight to avoid weight-related diseases, do it slowly and safely, focusing on changes you can happily maintain for life.

Eating foods with a low energy density can help fill you up while consuming fewer calories.

as fruits and veggies—have low energy density but take up a lot of space. This makes them more satisfying. In contrast, energy-dense foods pack a lot of calories into a small volume. For example, two cups (454 g) of baby carrots contain 70 calories; so do two tablespoons (28 g) of chocolate chips. Which seems more likely to fill you up?

Remember the food journal you kept before your doctor's visit? Keep using it. In addition to recording types and amounts of food, record their caloric content. Reference tables are available in bookstores, online, and as smartphone apps. Once you understand where the bulk of your calories come from, you'll be able to make low-cal substitutions without feeling as though you're starving.

NEEDING NUTRIENTS

You may have heard of an empty calorie. There is no such thing. Every calorie contributes to your energy intake. The best calories are high in nutrients, the building blocks your body needs to grow and function. Healthy eating involves balancing nutrient intake with counting calories. There are three major types of nutrients: carbohydrates, fats, and proteins.

Carbohydrates include sugar, starch, and fiber. They're found in fruits, grains, and processed foods containing flour or sugar. Look

LIQUID POISON

Between 1977 and 2001, average caloric intake from sugar-sweetened beverages increased by 135 percent.[2] Among teens, 67 percent of those calories came from soda.[3] Almost 25 percent of teens drank three or more sodas each day, the caloric equivalent of an extra meal.[4]

In North America, sodas and other sugary drinks are sweetened with high fructose corn syrup containing up to 55 percent fructose. Animal studies show high-fructose diets lead to increased energy intake, excess fat storage, and insulin resistance. Making matters worse, fructose does not suppress your body's production of ghrelin, the hormone that tells you you're hungry. As a result, you may overeat without realizing it.

for high-fiber carbs made from whole grains: these sources have more micronutrients and are slow to digest, so you'll feel full longer. On average, carbs contain four calories per gram.

Fats include saturated, unsaturated, trans fats, and cholesterol. Each gram of fat contains nine and one-half calories. This high calorie count is why low-fat diets are popular even though they're not more effective than simply reducing calories. More important than calorie content, however, is the type of fat you're eating. Unsaturated fats from plants and fish help regulate insulin sensitivity and blood cholesterol; saturated fats from meat, dairy, and eggs can raise your cholesterol. Avoid anything containing trans fats, which, according to the Institute of Medicine, "provide no known benefit to human health."[5]

Proteins include meats, fish, eggs, milk, and beans. Protein contains four calories per gram, but your body uses protein energy only as a last resort. Normally, proteins provide building materials for body structures and function. Choose those with the healthiest possible fat content.

For help establishing a healthy nutrient balance, consult a doctor or dietician. You can also visit www.choosemyplate.gov for American guidelines, or download the Canada Food Guide.

DECODING FOOD LABELS

A lot of the information you need to make healthful food choices is right on food packages. On a food label, calories are given for one serving. To get an accurate calorie count, check how many servings are in a package and how many servings make up your regular portion size.

Fat content appears as a total and is also broken down by type. If the amount listed under % Daily Value for saturated fats, trans fats, or cholesterol is 20 percent or more, don't eat it. Carbohydrates are listed as total, sugar, and fiber—any remaining grams come from starch. Look for high fiber, which is a % Daily Value greater than 20 percent. Remember sugar includes what's naturally in the food and what's added during manufacturing. In addition, compare the vitamin content to the recommended daily values of these important micronutrients.

PICKING A PROGRAM

If you decide to follow a structured diet or commercial weight-loss plan, make sure it promotes gradual weight loss of no more than two pounds (0.9 kg) per week. It should teach permanent lifestyle changes and encourage exercise. It should not make foods "bad" or "illegal." Avoid plans that exclude food groups. Do not choose a weight loss plan that makes outrageous, unsupported claims about how well it works.

Nutrition Facts

Serving Size 5 oz. (144g)
Servings Per Container 4

Amount Per Serving

Calories 310   **Calories** from Fat 100

% Daily Value*

Total Fat 15g	**21%**
Saturated Fat 2.6g	**17%**
Trans Fat 1g	
Cholesterol 118mg	**39%**
Sodium 560mg	**28%**
Total Carbohydrate 12g	**4%**
Dietary Fiber 1g	**4%**
Sugars 1g	
Protein 24g	

Vitamin A 1%	•	**Vitamin C** 2%
Calcium 2%	•	**Iron** 5%

*Percent Daily Values are based on a 2,000 calorie diet. Your daily values may be higher or lower depending on your calorie needs:

	Calories	2,000	2,500
Total Fat	Less Than	65g	80g
Saturated Fat	Less Than	20g	25g
Cholesterol	Less Than	300mg	300mg
Sodium	Less Than	2,400mg	2,400mg
Total Carbohydrate		300g	375g
Dietary Fiber		25g	30g

Calories per gram:
    Fat 9 • Carbohydrate 4 • Protein 4

This food has a lot of fat, cholesterol, and sodium.

Before eating a packaged food, read the ingredient list too. Components are listed in descending order of weight, but the vocabulary is sometimes misleading. For example, corn syrup, high fructose corn syrup, fruit juice concentrate, maltose, dextrose, sucrose, honey, and maple syrup all mean the same thing: added sugar. If one or more of these items is at the beginning of the ingredient list, avoid that food: it's high in sugar.

Manufacturers also brand products as "fat free," "whole grain," or "all natural," but that doesn't mean they're healthy—marshmallows are fat free! Always compare marketing claims to the food label and ingredient list before making your choice.

WHAT IF YOU CAN'T AFFORD TO EAT HEALTHFUL FOODS?

When treating obesity, doctors recommend replacing sugary, high-fat foods with fruits, veggies, whole grains, chicken, and fish. Unfortunately, these options often cost more than less-healthy alternatives. A 1999 United Kingdom study showed that women with the healthiest diets spent 617 pounds sterling (approximately $930) more on food each year.[6]

The cost of eating more healthfully has caused food insecurity in 11.9 percent of

Drinking water instead of drinks with sugar or calories is one quick lifestyle change.

American households. Food insecurity is the "limited or uncertain availability of nutritionally acceptable or safe foods."[7] Food insecurity promotes obesity, because families switch to lower-cost, less-nutritious foods before reducing the amount of food they consume. These inexpensive foods tend to have the highest energy densities.

Depending on your family's situation, nutritious choices may be difficult to afford. The problem may be worse if you also live in what is called a food desert—an urban area with poor access to supermarkets. As an alternative, find out whether reasonably priced fruits and vegetables are available through farmer's markets or community gardens, or grow your own in containers. Frozen fruits and vegetables are another option when fresh are unavailable or expensive. Choose varieties without added sauces, salt, or sugar. Use what you know about nutrition and food labels to make the healthiest possible selections from the choices available.

SMALL CHANGES AND SECRET TIPS

It will be easier to reach your healthy eating goals if you use Anna's strategy—mastering one change at a time. Here are some little differences that could make a big difference in your weight and your health:

- Drink water instead of sugar-sweetened beverages.
- Chew sugarless gum.
- Don't eat any processed food with more than five ingredients or any ingredients you can't pronounce.

- Don't eat directly from the package. Measuring a serving into a bowl helps control portion size.

- Home-cooked meals have fewer calories and more nutrients, so eat them whenever possible.

- Order from the kid's menu at fast-food restaurants. At sit-down places, take half your entrée home for tomorrow's lunch or dinner.

- Take healthful snacks when you leave the house.

- Have a plan for coping with food events such as birthdays and family reunions.

DERANGED AND DEADLY: A TIMELINE OF EARLY OBESITY TREATMENTS

Battling weight isn't new. Here are a few unhealthy highlights from humans' fight against obesity:

- **1880s: Gynecologist Howard Kelly attempted the first surgical removal of fat.**
- **1888: The Eat Your Food Slowly Society promoted the weight-loss benefits of thorough chewing.**
- **1900s: People deliberately swallowed pills containing tapeworms.**
- **1910: Tablets made of the poisons arsenic and strychnine were a trendy method for weight loss.**
- **1914: The Gardner Reducing Machine became the first mechanical massage device used to treat obesity.**
- **1936: Thousands of people took the industrial toxin dinitrophenol to speed up their metabolisms. In addition to accelerating weight loss, the drug caused rashes, loss of taste, cataracts, and death.**

- Pay with cash instead of a debit or credit card. You're less likely to buy an unhealthy treat when using real money.

- Retrain your brain. Never use food as a reward or punish yourself by denying it.

If you're feeling overwhelmed, take one step at a time. Remember, healthful eating doesn't mean you have to eliminate foods you love. Allow yourself a reasonable serving, and then offset the treat with high-nutrient, low-energy choices.

ASK YOURSELF THIS

- *What's the easiest single change you can make to cut excess calories from your diet?*

- *Do your current food choices provide a healthy balance of nutrients?*

- *Have you tried dieting in the past? How did you feel while following the program, and what happened when you stopped?*

- *Anna's goal is to master a figure skating jump. What could motivate you to follow a balanced diet?*

- *Which unhealthy foods are you most tempted by? Think of a healthful alternative you might be able to substitute.*

MAKING TIME TO MOVE

S ix months have passed since Austin found out he needed to lose weight to control his high blood pressure. Despite his reservations, modifying his diet was relatively painless, but Dr. Brownell insisted he exercise too. That was the part he really

Taking stairs instead of an elevator is a quick way to fit in a little extra exercise.

resisted. Austin thought exercise was painful and boring, and he was way too intimidated to hang around the muscleheads at the gym. Luckily, Dr. Brownell told him he didn't have to "exercise" to be active, he just had to move.

So Austin looked for creative ways to increase his activity at home. He started taking study breaks every half hour, walking around the room. Next, he volunteered to do housework, which made his mom happy. Then, he made a rule against watching television sitting down. At first, it was hard to follow his programs while doing soup-can bicep curls and marching in place, but after a little while, he barely noticed. Finally, he was ready to take things to the next level—literally.

Austin stood at the base of the staircase, looking up. His apartment was four flights up, and he couldn't remember the last time he was able to climb them all. Weeks ago, when he began working at it, he needed breaks on the first flight and had to take the elevator the rest of the way. But he had been getting stronger and fitter, and at last, he was ready to go all the way.

Austin put his foot on the first riser and started climbing. He moved steadily, deliberately. One flight . . . two . . . three . . . his breathing got a little rough halfway up the fourth flight, but he kept climbing. He could feel himself getting healthier, one step at a time.

HEALTHY MOVING

It's easier to avoid eating calories than to burn them off through physical activity. However, caloric restriction without exercise may cause your body to lose muscle as well as fat. Losing muscle mass lowers your BMR, making it harder to keep the weight off in the long run.

THE BIGGEST LOSERS

Due to severely restricted diets and punishing daily workouts, contestants on the television show *The Biggest Loser* achieve massive weight loss in a very short period of time. These are lifestyle changes most people can't reasonably sustain once they leave the show. Recently, Today.com interviewed contestants from the first 11 seasons, and approximately two-thirds had regained some or all of the weight lost on camera.[1] According to other contestants, the real portion of contestants who regained weight may be closer to 85 or 90 percent.[2]

Weight regain also results from the body's need to protect its energy reserves. A 2012 study showed that the body slows its BMR by up to 504 calories per day more during rapid weight loss than would be expected from the weight loss alone.[3] As a result, as Dr. Yoni Freedhoff of the University of Ottawa noted, "The biggest losers each and every season aren't in fact the contestants, they're the viewers. . . . Viewers are being taught nonsustainable approaches to weight management."[3] One indication the show fosters unrealistic expectations is the contestants' disappointment at losing "only" four or five pounds (1.8 or 2.3 kg) a week, when doctors recommend a maximum of two pounds (0.9 kg).

Another great reason to get active is that exercise improves your health even if you don't lose much weight. Physical activity decreases your risk for heart problems and can even reverse insulin resistance. Overweight people who exercise regularly often have a lower risk of premature death than lean people who are sedentary.

TYPES OF EXERCISE

Exercises are categorized according to their effect on your body's metabolism: aerobic and anaerobic. During aerobic exercise, your cells produce energy by using oxygen to burn sugar. Aerobic exercises use large muscle groups, like the ones in your legs, and can be comfortably continued for 30 minutes or more. Examples include walking, biking, swimming, dancing, team sports, and vacuuming. These exercises are great for your heart, and they burn more stored energy than anaerobic alternatives.

If your muscles work so hard they run out of oxygen, they switch to anaerobic energy metabolism—the kind that makes you "feel the burn." The body can only sustain this level of work for a few minutes, so you won't burn as many calories doing anaerobic exercises. However, because they encourage muscle growth, they increase your BMR. That means you'll burn more calories just lying down—a bonus that helps keep lost weight from coming back.

Anaerobic exercises are also called strength, resistance, or weight training. Austin's soup-can bicep curls are a good example, as are rock climbing, strenuous gardening, and weight machines at the gym. Effective anaerobic strength training involves a certain amount of force, increasing your risk of injury. Pay close attention to proper form, and if possible, find an expert who can train you to do the exercises safely.

CHOOSE YOUR OWN ADVENTURE

There are 3,500 calories in one pound (0.5 kg) of fat. Losing weight at a healthy rate of one pound per week therefore requires an energy deficit of 500 calories per day. In one hour, a 200-pound (91 kg) person can burn a range of calories, depending on the activity:

- ballroom dancing: 273 calories
- bicycling slower than ten miles per hour (16 kmh): 364 calories
- bowling: 273 calories
- ice-skating: 637 calories
- playing basketball: 728 calories
- swimming laps: 528 calories
- walking at two miles per hour (3.2 kmh): 255 calories

You can improve your health without living at the gym—babysitting, yard work, and walking the dog all contribute to your total physical activity. Try taking the stairs instead of the elevator, and park farther from buildings to increase the distance you have to walk.

Lifting weights is a form of anaerobic exercise.

GOALS AND HOW TO REACH THEM

For teens, experts recommend at least 60 minutes of physical activity most days of the week, pushing hard enough to sweat. If you've always been sedentary, you probably won't be able to meet these guidelines when you begin. Follow Austin's example by setting small goals and working your way up. Use these tips to get started and stick with it:

- If you're obese, you may have trouble moving the way a slender teen does. Before starting a new physical activity, ask your doctor whether you're healthy enough to do it safely.

- You don't have to complete all 60 minutes in a single session. Break it into shorter segments throughout the day. Any additional movement burns calories.

- If you're not used to exercising, you might not like it at first. Persevere! Studies show the more active you become, the more you'll enjoy physical activity.

- Alternate between aerobic and anaerobic exercise, and vary the type of activity. This reduces boredom and gives your body time to recover, reducing your risk of injury.

- You're most likely to keep active if you choose exercises that are pain-free, convenient, and fun.

- Set specific goals and track your progress in your journal. When you reach a milestone, celebrate. You've earned it!

KEEPING IT OFF

The National Weight Control Registry tracks more than 5,000 people who've lost an average of 66 pounds (29.9 kg) and kept it off for 5.5 years. Here's what they have in common:

- Television: 62 percent watch less than ten hours each week.
- Weighing in: 78 percent weigh themselves at least once a week.
- Breakfast: 78 percent eat this meal every day.
- Exercise: 90 percent do this an average of 60 minutes a day.
- Eating habit: 98 percent continue eating a healthy diet.
- Living better: 100 percent say their quality of life is higher since they lost weight.[4]

ASK YOURSELF THIS

- *What opportunities for physical activity are freely available to you?*

- *How can you make getting active convenient and fun?*

- *Think of a physical activity, such as dancing or rock climbing, that you would love to learn or be able to do. What changes would you have to make to reach that goal?*

- *If you don't want to sacrifice your screen time, how can you make that time more active?*

VIDEO GAMES CAN BE GOOD FOR YOU

Because people are more likely to exercise if they're having fun, scientists are investigating the health benefits of "exergames"—video games that require a physical component. With a few exceptions, exergames require less exertion than traditional exercises such as walking on a treadmill. However, exergames burn more calories than sedentary gaming, making them better for your health. Some people also enjoy these games more than traditional exercise, making participation more sustainable over the long term.

BEYOND DIET AND EXERCISE

Matteo tied the hospital gown around his neck and climbed onto the gurney. They would be coming for him soon, and he was starting to sweat from nervousness. But he wouldn't change his mind now.

Bariatric surgery is an option for people who are very obese and unable to lose weight by other means.

His parents pushed through the curtains. Mom squeezed his hand while Dad patted him on the shoulder, clearly holding back tears. They had supported him all along, even changing their own diets and brainstorming physical activities they could do as a family. It wasn't their fault he couldn't lose weight. It wasn't his fault, either. He followed his doctor's instructions to the letter and even took a medication with some embarrassing side effects, but it didn't make enough difference. Sometimes, Matteo felt like his body doesn't want him to be healthy. That's why he agreed to try bariatric surgery, despite the risks. He didn't want to be the first kid in his family whose parents would outlive him.

A nurse shooed them back out to the waiting room, and Matteo lay back on the thin pillow, thinking about the ways his life was about to change. He couldn't imagine making a meal out of a single tablespoon of food—he used to put that much ketchup on every burger! He knew he'd get used to it somehow, like he got used to everything else. Finally being healthy would be worth it all, and if he could lose enough weight, he might even find the guts to ask Laura to the senior prom. Matteo was so busy picturing the corsage he would buy her he didn't even feel the needle when the nurse inserted the IV.

WHEN LIFESTYLE ISN'T ENOUGH

Lifestyle changes are the cornerstone of obesity treatment for teens, because the healthy habits you develop now will carry you through life. In addition, the complex changes your body experiences during adolescence, and the increased risk your developing brain might lead you to ignore your doctor's recommendations, make medical interventions especially dangerous.

If healthful eating and exercise aren't enough to improve your weight-related diseases, however, your doctor could decide the benefits of medical treatments outweigh the risks. It's important you understand the potential risks and benefits so you can make an informed decision.

MEDICATION

Since the 1930s, approximately one dozen different drugs have been approved for weight loss in the United States. All but three have been withdrawn due to dangerous side effects such as heart defects and stroke.

As of 2013, only orlistat has been approved for use in teens. However, the American Association of Pediatrics recommends orlistat (also known by the trade name Xenical) only for teens with BMIs at or above the 99th percentile. That's because orlistat can cause vitamin deficiencies that interfere with growth and health.

When you're taking orlistat, your intestines absorb only approximately 30 percent of the fat in your food.[1] The other 70 percent is expelled as waste, leading to side effects such as urgent bowel movements, gas, and stool leakage. Most patients minimize these effects by eating a reduced-fat diet, but the less fat you consume, the less impact orlistat will have on your weight. On average, patients taking orlistat lose an extra five to seven pounds (2.3 to 3.2 kg) over the course of one to two years.[2]

You may have heard of Alli, a low-dose version of orlistat available without a prescription. Alli is only approved for use by adults. If you're under 18, don't take any form of orlistat without your doctor's supervision.

A PROMISING NEW DRUG

The medication metformin is used to manage T2D in kids and teens. It's not currently approved for treating obesity, but clinical trials for this application are underway. In a study conducted in the United Kingdom, taking metformin daily reduced kids' BMIs from 37.1 to 36.56 over six months of treatment.[3] More important, risk factors for T2D also decreased, suggesting metformin might help prevent weight-related disease.

THE INS AND OUTS OF BARIATRIC SURGERY

If your health is in danger and all other obesity treatments have failed, your doctor might suggest bariatric surgery. There are no long-term studies tracking the effects of this surgery on teens, so for safety reasons, it's considered a last resort. Doctors also disagree on appropriate indications for surgery, but you may be a candidate if you meet several criteria:

- You're BMI is greater than 50 and you're healthy, or you're BMI is greater than 40 and you have weight-related diseases.

- You've tried to lose weight for at least six months without success.

- You're fully grown—ages 13 to 14 for girls or 15 to 16 for boys.

- You're psychologically healthy and able to make rational, logical decisions.

- You have a supportive family environment.

- You're committed to following post-surgery requirements for lifestyle and nutrition.

- If you're female, you will not become pregnant for at least two years.

Two types of bariatric surgery are currently being performed for teens. In laparoscopic banding, surgeons use small incisions and a camera to place a band around the upper part

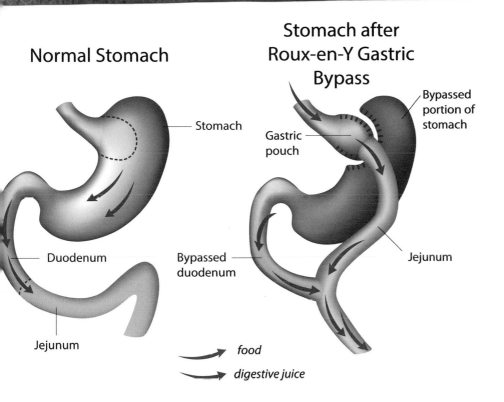

Normal Stomach

- Stomach
- Duodenum
- Jejunum

Stomach after Roux-en-Y Gastric Bypass

- Bypassed portion of stomach
- Gastric pouch
- Bypassed duodenum
- Jejunum

→ food

→ digestive juice

of the stomach. The band restricts the amount of food the stomach can hold. This procedure is usually less effective for weight loss than other surgical techniques, but its advantages for young people are that it's reversible and less likely to interfere with nutrient absorption. Doctors have used laparoscopic banding on Australian and European teens with good results. American teens have to be 18 to qualify for the procedure.

Roux-en-Y gastric bypass, sometimes known as stomach stapling, was developed in the 1960s. After the Roux-en-Y gastric bypass procedure is performed, digestion mostly bypasses the stomach. During this procedure, surgeons create a small pouch at the top of the stomach that they connect to the jejunum, the middle portion of the small intestine. Following surgery, one tablespoon of food is enough to make the patient feel full. However, because that food bypasses the duodenum, the first part of the small intestine, the patient will have trouble absorbing certain nutrients. To compensate, that person will have to take supplements for the rest of his or her life. To avoid a side effect known as dumping syndrome, he or she will have to be careful to not consume sugars and starches.

For teens, other side effects of both surgeries may include low bone density from poor vitamin and mineral absorption, gallstones,

GENE THERAPY FOR WEIGHT LOSS

Adiponectin is a hormone that decreases with increasing body fat. Low levels are associated with insulin resistance, so increasing adiponectin concentration might be a way to prevent diseases such as T2D from developing.

A group of researchers at the University of Alberta in Canada injected an extra copy of the adiponectin gene into the muscle cells of mice. Then, they fed the mice a high-calorie, 44.9 percent fat diet to test the effect. Five weeks later, mice that received gene therapy weighed significantly less than untreated mice that also ate high-fat food.

Gene therapy for human obesity won't be available anytime soon, but Dr. Jason Dyck, the head mouse researcher, said, "I think our finding may bring this treatment one step closer to clinical trials [with humans]."[4]

After bariatric surgery, you must commit to the required lifestyle changes.

and ulcers. In addition, girls have an increased risk of pregnancy because weight loss improves ovulation and enhanced self-esteem increases the chance they'll take sexual risks. And death is possible in up to five out of 1,000 patients.[5]

LIFE AFTER SURGERY

If you're considering surgery, you need to recognize weight loss is not guaranteed. Good results require committing to physical activity; small, well-balanced, highly nutritious meals; and frequent follow-ups with your doctor. Parents of teens who've opted for surgery say their kids have trouble sticking with the strict lifestyle and supplement regimes necessary after the procedure.

Patients who accept these restrictions, however, lose 50 percent or more of their stored fat.[6] They also report improved self-esteem, better social relationships, and the reversal of diseases associated with obesity.

Research on adult patients shows bariatric surgery also reduces the brain's reward

COMPLEMENTARY MEDICINE

Complementary medicine is defined as "the use and practice of therapies or diagnostic techniques that may not be part of any current Western health care system, culture, or society."[7] One of these is hypnosis, the creation of a trance state. The trance allows the therapist to make suggestions that support the patient's behavioral changes.

You're probably most familiar with the kind of hypnosis that makes ordinary people quack like a duck or cluck like a chicken. Hypnosis has serious applications and is being studied for the treatment of obesity. In general, hypnosis for weight loss is ineffectual. Research shows, however, that hypnosis for stress relief leads to significant weight loss over a period of 18 months.

Acupuncture involves inserting fine needles into specific points on the body. Developed in China, it is one of the oldest known medical treatments, and Western scientists are beginning to recognize its usefulness. In rats, acupuncture helps the brain suppress appetite. Animal studies also show acupuncture affects hormone levels, insulin sensitivity, and cholesterol.

Scientific evidence for acupuncture in humans is mixed, but many studies suggest it encourages weight loss. Like all treatments for obesity, acupuncture works best when combined with diet and exercise.

response to images of food, suggesting deep physiological changes following the procedure. If these benefits are significant enough to make surgery a good choice for you, take the time to research hospitals and surgeons with experience treating teen patients before you commit.

ASK YOURSELF THIS

- *Would the small additional weight loss orlistat provides be worth enduring its side effects?*

- *How much weight would you have to lose to make the risks and requirements of surgery acceptable?*

- *If you're already struggling with the lifestyle changes required for nonsurgical weight loss, could you accept the stricter regime required post surgery?*

- *If you're experiencing social stigma as a consequence of your weight, do you think it would get better or worse after surgery?*

COPING AND SUPPORT

The house was quiet after midnight. Ashley was alone in her room, her glowing monitor the only source of light. The garbage can beside her desk was full of crinkled, empty wrappers.

It started with the chemistry test. Ashley studied all week, but she knew she was in trouble as soon as she flipped over the first page. There was no way she passed, and if she couldn't get her grade up, she'd never get accepted to college. Then, after school, she had a nasty fight with her parents over the chores she'd neglected while fruitlessly studying. The final straw was another dateless Friday night. Despite the weight she had lost over the last year, Ashley still didn't have a boyfriend.

She knew she shouldn't eat the leftover Halloween candy, but it was there and she just couldn't stop herself. And the chocolate really did help, at least for a little while. But soon, she felt heartsick and disgusted with herself, like she had thrown all her hard work away.

Ashley logged on to her favorite support group, fingers flying as she posted the whole depressing story. Within minutes, a girl from Australia replied. Kids from Canada and Europe quickly joined the thread, and every one of them had stories about days like Ashley's. They sent her cyber hugs and told her not to give up, and soon they were swapping tips for getting back on track.

It was almost two o'clock when she finally shut down the computer, but Ashley didn't care. She'd be able to sleep, and she knew she'd wake up more determined than ever. She realized one bad day didn't have to erase all the progress that came before. If other kids could do it, she could, too.

ADAPTED FOR THE WRONG ENVIRONMENT

Throughout the vast majority of human history, food was scarce and we had to work really hard to get it. As a result, our bodies are programmed to stockpile energy in case famine strikes. These days, however, few people in the Western world ever truly go without. We have

ADDICTED TO FOOD

As far as your brain is concerned, there's very little difference between overeating and methamphetamines. Unlike drug addicts, however, you can't manage your addiction by eliminating food from your environment. A better strategy involves limiting consumption of the most strongly addicting foods, including chocolate and chocolate milkshakes, french fries, pizza, salty snacks, sugared breakfast cereals, and baked goods. In general, dairy products and any foods with processed fats and flours are triggers.

Sugars, starches, and refined white flour have a high glycemic index—after you eat them, your blood sugar rises dramatically. This spike in blood sugar appears to trigger addictive responses, so avoid such foods whenever possible. Addictive foods are also most powerful when eaten in combination, such as at fast-food restaurants.

easy access to energy-dense foods—precisely the kinds we've adapted to crave—and their abundance has increased so quickly we haven't had time to evolve.

When lifestyle changes cause your body to burn fat, the concentration of leptin in your blood decreases. As a result, your brain believes you're starving. It panics, slowing your metabolism and increasing your appetite. This hardwired response is designed to restore energy reserves to their previous level, and research shows that even if you maintain your weight loss for ten years, your brain will continue fighting to reestablish your former set point.

In other words, your body and brain will work against you for the rest of your life. Even though it's very difficult, you can outsmart them both.

DON'T EAT THE MARSHMALLOW

In 1968, psychologist Walter Mischel offered four-year-old kids a choice: eat one marshmallow now, or wait 15 minutes and get two. Few children—approximately 30 percent—held out the full 15 minutes, and most gave up in less than three.[1]

New research shows that kids who can't delay gratification—choosing small, immediate

*Identify behaviors you want to change
and decide how to measure success.*

rewards rather than waiting for large ones that
aren't guaranteed—are more likely to become
obese. Therefore, improving self-control
and learning to focus on long-term goals are
essential to achieving weight loss.

The critical skill is your ability to redirect
your attention. During the marshmallow test,
successful kids distracted themselves by closing
their eyes, playing under the desk, or singing
songs. Not thinking about the treat gave them

the power to resist it. You can use the same technique to overcome temptations during weight loss: develop a distraction strategy to implement when you're swayed by foods or activities inconsistent with your goals. Doing this consistently takes practice, but identifying healthy rewards you can substitute for unhealthy alternatives will help.

SETTING GOALS AND MAKING PLANS

Improving your health through weight loss is an enormous, overwhelming task. Without a plan, you're very likely to become discouraged and quit. Increase your odds for success by focusing on small, sequential changes that are 100 percent achievable. The SMART method is one approach to goal setting, and its name comes from the first letter of words that can help keep you on track:

- Identify a **specific** behavior you want to change: for example, drinking water instead of soda.

- Decide how to **measure** your success: record every beverage in a food journal.

- Make your goal **action-based**, and use strong verbs to define it: "I will drink water," not "I'll try to avoid soda."

- Be **realistic** about your capabilities and preferences: if you're currently drinking soda every day, cut out one a week instead of going cold turkey.

- Make it **timely** by setting a schedule: you're less likely to cheat if you're facing a deadline.

- When you've reached your first goal, reward yourself! Then, set a new one and immediately begin working toward it.

Studies show that for many obese people, improved quality of life is more important than reducing long-term health risks. As a result, you'll be more motivated if you focus on the kind of life you want to lead rather than shooting for a number on the scale. To be successful, sometimes you have to change your definition of success.

TEN THOUSAND STEPS TO A HEALTHIER YOU

Looking for an easy way to track your physical activity? Try measuring steps with a pedometer. As with all exercise, start with what's comfortable for you. Work your way up to 10,000 steps a day, the rough equivalent of 60 minutes of exercise. Check if your local library has pedometers to loan.

WHEN YOU NEED SUPPORT

If you're like most teens, you live at home and have limited control over groceries and meal planning. Meeting your health goals will therefore be easier if you have your family's support. This may involve changing the diet and activity patterns of your entire household, and sacrificing their favorite indulgences may cause parents or siblings to resent you. To reduce this backlash, be sure to tell your family how you feel, what you need, and how important they are to your success.

In addition to family support, research shows that frequent contact with your health-care team improves your odds of achieving a healthy weight. Find doctors, nutritionists, or personal trainers who will provide encouragement in addition to the education and resources you'll need.

At some point in your journey, you'll probably want the support of teens who know exactly what you're going through. If you've got friends who are obese, join forces to celebrate

MAKING RIPPLES

One reason unhealthy behaviors are difficult to change is because they often reinforce each other. You can use these complementary relationships to your advantage. If you always eat while watching television, reducing your screen time will automatically reduce calories. Starting a meal with a high-nutrient, low-energy salad will cause you to feel full sooner, automatically decreasing the amount of energy-dense steak and baked potato you'll eat. Try exercising with a friend to make a workout feel like a treat. Look for other complementary associations in your daily routines, and make small lifestyle changes that will create the biggest ripples.

Remember your family and friends love you, and you deserve to be loved no matter your size.

successes and minimize setbacks. There may also be free local support groups you can join or online communities that will be there when you need them.

A NEW BEGINNING

An unfortunate reality is that 95 to 98 percent of people regain weight after short-term dieting.[2] You are most likely to be in this group if your goal is to change your appearance. Focus instead on improving your health, and don't make lifestyle changes you're not prepared to maintain indefinitely.

Remember that the greatest health benefits of obesity treatments accompany the first 10 percent of body weight lost.[3] And remind yourself that 10 percent may also be enough to dramatically improve your mobility, self-confidence, and overall satisfaction with life.

Living with obesity will never be easy. But you have the power to make it a whole lot better.

ASK YOURSELF THIS

- *Will it be hard to convince your family to support your lifestyle changes? What can you do if it is difficult to persuade them?*

- *Who will you go to when you're discouraged?*

- *Would you be more comfortable joining a face-to-face support group or one that meets online?*

- *What are your strongest unhealthy addictions? What strategies can you implement to resist them?*

- *If you improve your health without losing significant body fat, will you be satisfied or disappointed?*

JUST THE FACTS

Obesity is an unhealthy excess of body fat, measured using body mass index, or BMI (kg/m2).

A BMI equal to or greater than the 85th percentile among teens of the same age and gender is overweight; a BMI equal or greater than the 95th percentile is obese.

As of 2012, 32 percent of American kids and teens were overweight or obese, and the prevalence of obesity was rising.

Obesity is caused by complex interactions between genetic and environmental factors, such as access to abundant, inexpensive calories and increased sedentary behaviors.

Childhood and adolescent obesity are risk factors for weight-related diseases such as asthma, type 2 diabetes, heart disease, stroke, and cancer.

Visceral fat is more closely linked to medical complications than obesity in general.

Weight stigma and bullying are usually the first negative consequences of teen obesity.

Weight-based teasing is a risk factor for low self-esteem, anxiety and depression, eating disorders, and suicide.

Doctors use BMI, body scans, waist-to-hip ratios, and blood tests to determine whether a person's weight is affecting his or her health.

Because losing weight is very difficult, many experts believe preventing obesity is of utmost importance and needs to begin before birth.

Healthy eating and physical activity are the foundation of all medical treatments for obesity, and these lifestyle changes are most effective when maintained indefinitely.

Weight loss of one to two pounds (0.5 to 0.9 kg) per week is safer and more sustainable than rapid rates promoted by reality shows such as *The Biggest Loser*.

Orlistat is the only prescription medication approved for use in teens with obesity.

There are no long-term studies on the impact of bariatric surgery for teens with obesity, so it's usually a treatment of last resort.

Losing 10 percent of your baseline body weight is enough to significantly improve your medical health and quality of life.

WHERE TO TURN

If You're Concerned Your Weight Is Affecting Your Health

Visit http://apps.nccd.cdc.gov/dnpabmi/ and enter your date of birth, date of measurement, sex, height, and weight. The calculator will determine your BMI and compare it to those of comparable teens. If you're near the 85th percentile for your age and gender, or you're experiencing weight-related symptoms, contact your doctor. He or she will assess your risk of disease and work with you to develop a treatment plan. Remember many weight-related diseases have no symptoms in the early stages. Catching and treating these diseases early can significantly decrease your risk of developing serious health problems.

If You or Someone You Know Is Being Bullied

If family members are a source of stigma, tell them how their attitudes are affecting you. When stigma comes from peers, talk to your family, school counselor, or other trusted adult. Face bullies by standing up tall, staying calm, and avoiding escalating the situation. If bullying is affecting your mental health, see your doctor for medical support, or visit the American Academy of Child & Adolescent Psychiatry at www.aacap.org to find a counselor or psychologist near you.

If you or someone you know is thinking of suicide, act immediately—tell a trusted adult, or call 1-800-SUICIDE, the Boys Town National Hotline (1-800-448-3000), or Kid's Help Phone (1-800-668-6868, in Canada). To learn more about weight stigma and how you can advocate against it, visit the Yale Rudd Center for Food Policy & Obesity at www.yaleruddcenter.org or the International Size Acceptance Association at www.size-acceptance.org.

If You Need Information on Making Healthy Lifestyle Changes

Sorting through the conflicting advice on weight loss can be confusing and overwhelming. If you're looking for advice on nutrition, visit www.calorieking.com, www.choosemyplate.gov, or www.webmd.com. For inspiration to get active, check out www.americaonthemove.org, the National Association for Health and Fitness at www.physicalfitness.org, or Walking School Bus at www.walkingschoolbus.org.

Consult nutritionists and personal trainers for personalized recommendations. But before making any lifestyle changes, discuss them with your doctor to ensure they're sensible and safe for your current level of health.

If You're Considering Bariatric Surgery

Bariatric surgery is risky, and the lifestyle changes it demands are challenging for many teens to abide by. If you're considering surgery, make sure you know exactly what's involved and how having the procedure will affect your life. Visit the Mayo Clinic at www.mayoclinic.com, the Obesity Action Coalition at www.obesityaction.org, or www.weightlosssurgery.ca. Discuss your questions and concerns with your doctor, and when choosing a surgeon, look for one with experience treating teen patients.

If You Need Support

A supportive environment can make a big difference in your success, including meeting your weight-loss goals. Test drive teens-only online support groups until you find one that's right for you. The sites www.caloriesperhour.com and www.blubberbuster.com have teens-only discussion boards.

GLOSSARY

dumping syndrome
A side effect of gastric bypass surgery involving sweating, dizziness, pain, low blood pressure, and other symptoms caused by reduced ability to process and absorb starch and sugar.

energy density
The number of calories contained in a given volume of food.

energy imbalance
A difference—positive or negative—between the number of calories consumed and the number required by the body.

globesity
The rapid and widespread increase in obesity rates around the world, most likely caused by increased availability of energy-dense foods.

glycogen
A substance stored in the liver and muscles before being broken down to glucose and used for fuel.

leptin
A hormone secreted by adipocytes used to signal changes in the body's energy reserves.

metabolic syndrome
A series of hormonal and metabolic changes occurring with obesity that lead to weight-related diseases such as type 2 diabetes and heart disease.

metabolism
Chemical processes inside the body that control energy use and storage.

micronutrient
A vitamin and or mineral used by the body that occurs in low concentrations in foods.

portion
The number of food servings eaten at one time.

serving
An amount of food product labels specify and list corresponding calorie content and nutritional value.

set point
A level of stored energy the brain considers normal and works hard to maintain.

stigma
Negative judgments about a person's character based solely on weight or appearance.

subcutaneous
Beneath the skin.

visceral
Surrounding the internal organs.

ADDITIONAL RESOURCES

SELECTED BIBLIOGRAPHY

Bagchi, Debasis, and Harry G. Preuss, eds. *Obesity: Epidemiology, Pathophysiology, and Prevention*. 2nd ed. New York: CRC, 2013. Print.

Daniels, Stephen R. "The Consequences of Childhood Overweight and Obesity." *The Future of Children* 16.1 (2006): 47–67. Print.

Hoffman, John, Judith A. Salerno, and Alexandra Moss. *The Weight of the Nation: To Win We Have to Lose*. New York: St. Martin's, 2012. Print.

Puhl, Rebecca M., and Janet D. Latner. "Stigma, Obesity, and the Health of the Nation's Children." *Psychological Bulletin* 133.4 (2007): 557–580. Print.

FURTHER READINGS

LeBaron, Tyler, Jack Branson, and Mary Branson. *Cutting Myself in Half: 150 Pounds Lost One Byte at a Time*. Deerfield Beach, FL: Health Communications, 2009. Print.

Stettler, Nicolas, and Susan Shelly. *Living With Obesity*. New York: Facts on File, 2009. Print.

WEB SITES

To learn more about living with obesity, visit ABDO Publishing Company online at **www.abdopublishing.com**. Web sites about living with obesity are featured on our Book Links page. These links are routinely monitored and updated to provide the most current information available.

SOURCE NOTES

CHAPTER 1. THE SKINNY ON FAT: DEFINING OBESITY

1. John Hoffman, Judith A. Salerno, and Alexandra Moss. *The Weight of the Nation: To Win We Have to Lose.* New York: St. Martin's, 2012. Print. 11.

2. Debasis Bagchi and Harry G. Preuss, eds. *Obesity: Epidemiology, Pathophysiology, and Prevention.* New York: CRC, 2013. Print. 20.

3. Ibid. 3.

4. "Obesity and Overweight." *World Health Organization Media Centre.* World Health Organization, Mar. 2013. Web. 7 Aug. 2013.

5. Ibid.

6. Andrew M. Prentice. "The Emerging Epidemic of Obesity in Developing Countries." *International Journal of Epidemiology* 35 (2006): 93. Print.

7. "About BMI for Children and Teens." *Centers for Disease Control and Prevention.* CDC, 13 Sept. 2011. Web. 7 Aug. 2013.

8. "BMI Percentile Calculator for Child and Teen." *Centers for Disease Control and Prevention.* CDC, n.d. Web. 7 Aug. 2013.

CHAPTER 2. GANGING UP: NATURE, NURTURE, AND YOU

1. John Hoffman, Judith A. Salerno, and Alexandra Moss. *The Weight of the Nation: To Win We Have to Lose.* New York: St. Martin's, 2012. Print. 35.

2. Melania Manco and Bruno Dallapiccola. "Genetics of Pediatric Obesity." *Pediatrics* 130.1 (2012): 127. Print.

3. Debasis Bagchi and Harry G. Preuss, eds. *Obesity: Epidemiology, Pathophysiology, and Prevention.* New York: CRC, 2013. Print. 277.

4. Melania Manco and Bruno Dallapiccola. "Genetics of Pediatric Obesity." *Pediatrics* 130.1 (2012): 127. Print.

5. Youfa Wang and May A. Beydoun. "The Obesity Epidemic in the United States." *Epidemiological Reviews* 29 (2007): 24. Print.

6. Francis Delpeuch, et al. *Globesity: A Planet Out of Control.* London: Earthscan, 2009. Print. xvi.

7. John Hoffman, Judith A. Salerno, and Alexandra Moss. *The Weight of the Nation: To Win We Have to Lose.* New York: St. Martin's, 2012. Print. 33.

8. Debasis Bagchi and Harry G. Preuss, eds. *Obesity: Epidemiology, Pathophysiology, and Prevention.* New York: CRC, 2013. Print. 61.

9. John Hoffman, Judith A. Salerno, and Alexandra Moss. *The Weight of the Nation: To Win We Have to Lose.* New York: St. Martin's, 2012. Print. 41.

10. John Hoffman, Judith A. Salerno, and Alexandra Moss. *The Weight of the Nation: To Win We Have to Lose.* New York: St. Martin's, 2012. Print. 83.

11. Ibid. 122.

12. Debasis Bagchi and Harry G. Preuss, eds. *Obesity: Epidemiology, Pathophysiology, and Prevention.* New York: CRC, 2013. Print. 854.

13. John Hoffman, Judith A. Salerno, and Alexandra Moss. *The Weight of the Nation: To Win We Have to Lose.* New York: St. Martin's, 2012. Print. 134.

14. Youfa Wang and May A. Beydoun. "The Obesity Epidemic in the United States." *Epidemiological Reviews* 29 (2007): 19. Print.

15. Amanda S. Bruce, et al. "Brain Responses to Food Logos in Obese and Healthy Weight Children." *Journal of Pediatrics* 162 (2013): 759. Print.

16. John Hoffman, Judith A. Salerno, and Alexandra Moss. *The Weight of the Nation: To Win We Have to Lose*. New York: St. Martin's, 2012. Print. 106.

17. Francis Delpeuch, et al. *Globesity: A Planet Out of Control*. London: Earthscan, 2009. Print. 85.

CHAPTER 3. OBESITY IS BAD FOR YOUR HEALTH

1. Earl S. Ford. "The Epidemiology of Obesity and Asthma." *Journal of Allergy and Clinical Immunology* 115.5 (2005): 907. Print.

2. Rita de Cássia Ribeiro Silva, et al. "The Prevalence of Wheezing and Its Association With Body Mass Index and Abdominal Obesity in Children." *Journal of Asthma* 50.3 (2013): 270. Print.

3. Debasis Bagchi and Harry G. Preuss, eds. Obesity: *Epidemiology, Pathophysiology, and Prevention*. New York: CRC, 2013. Print. 952.

4. Debasis Bagchi and Harry G. Preuss, eds. *Obesity: Epidemiology, Pathophysiology, and Prevention*. New York: CRC, 2013. Print. 893.

5. Ibid. 215.

6. Ibid. 38.

7. Ram Weiss, Andrew A. Bremer, and Robert H. Lustig. "What Is Metabolic Syndrome, and Why Are Children Getting It?" *Annals of the New York Academy of Sciences* 1281 (2013): 123. Print.

8. Claire Friedemann, et al. "Cardiovascular Disease Risk in Healthy Children and Its Association With Body Mass Index." *British Medical Journal* 345 (2012): 4. Print.

9. William H. Dietz. "Health Consequences of Obesity in Youth." *Pediatrics* 101 (1998): 521. Print.

10. Claire Friedemann, et al. "Cardiovascular Disease Risk in Healthy Children and Its Association With Body Mass Index." *British Medical Journal* 345 (2012): 3. Print.

11. Ram Weiss, Andrew A. Bremer, and Robert H. Lustig. "What Is Metabolic Syndrome, and Why Are Children Getting It?" *Annals of the New York Academy of Sciences* 1281 (2013): 123. Print.

12. "Cancer and Obesity." *Fact Sheets*. Obesity Society, n.d. Web. 7 Aug. 2013.

13. John Hoffman, Judith A. Salerno, and Alexandra Moss. *The Weight of the Nation: To Win We Have to Lose*. New York: St. Martin's, 2012. Print. 19.

14. Claire Friedemann, et al. "Cardiovascular Disease Risk in Healthy Children and Its Association With Body Mass Index." *British Medical Journal* 345 (2012): 4. Print.

15. "Obesity Statistics." *Educational Resources*. Obesity Action Coalition, n.d. Web. 7 Aug. 2013.

16. "Obesity and Overweight." *World Health Organization Media Centre*. World Health Organization, Mar. 2013. Web. 7 Aug. 2013.

17. Jonathan Bor. "Study Details How Fat Costs Years." *Baltimore Sun*. Baltimore Sun, 8 Jan. 2003. Web. 7 Aug. 2013.

SOURCE NOTES CONTINUED

18. John Hoffman, Judith A. Salerno, and Alexandra Moss. *The Weight of the Nation: To Win We Have to Lose.* New York: St. Martin's, 2012. Print. 21.

19. J. J. Reilly, et al. "Health Consequences of Obesity." *Archives of Disease in Childhood* 88 (2003): 751. Print.

20. Ram Weiss, Andrew A. Bremer, and Robert H. Lustig. "What Is Metabolic Syndrome, and Why Are Children Getting It?" *Annals of the New York Academy of Sciences* 1281 (2013): 124. Print.

CHAPTER 4. THE UGLY TRUTH ABOUT WEIGHT STIGMA

1. K. S. O'Brien, J. D. Latner, and J. A. Hunter. "Obesity Discrimination." *International Journal of Obesity* 37 (2013): 455. Print.

2. Sean Levinson. "Abercrombie & Fitch CEO Explains Why He Hates Fat Chicks." *Elite Daily.* Elite Daily, 3 May 2013. Web. 7 Aug. 2013.

3. Rebecca M. Puhl and Janet D. Latner. "Stigma, Obesity, and the Health of the Nation's Children." *Psychological Bulletin* 133.4 (2007): 563. Print.

4. Ibid. 564.

5. Rebecca M. Puhl, et al. "Weight Stigmatization and Bias Reduction." *Health Education Research* 23.2 (2008): 351. Print.

6. Andrew M. Prentice. "The Emerging Epidemic of Obesity in Developing Countries." *International Journal of Epidemiology* 35 (2006): 96. Print.

7. Rebecca M. Puhl and Janet D. Latner. "Stigma, Obesity, and the Health of the Nation's Children." *Psychological Bulletin* 133.4 (2007): 559. Print.

8. Rebecca A. Krukowski, et al. "Overweight Children, Weight-Based Teasing and Academic Performance." *International Journal of Pediatric Obesity* 4 (2009): 278. Print.

9. Jeanne Walsh Pierce and Jane Wardle. "Cause and Effect Beliefs and Self-Esteem of Overweight Children." *Journal of Child Psychology & Psychiatry* 38.6 (1997): 648. Print.

10. Ibid. 649.

11. Debasis Bagchi and Harry G. Preuss, eds. *Obesity: Epidemiology, Pathophysiology, and Prevention.* New York: CRC, 2013. Print. 26.

12. Rebecca M. Puhl and Janet D. Latner. "Stigma, Obesity, and the Health of the Nation's Children." *Psychological Bulletin* 133.4 (2007): 567. Print.

CHAPTER 5. AN OUNCE OF PREVENTION, A POUND OF CURE

1. John Hoffman, Judith A. Salerno, and Alexandra Moss. *The Weight of the Nation: To Win We Have to Lose.* New York: St. Martin's, 2012. Print. 127.

2. "What Every Family Can Do: The 5-2-1-0 Rule." *Childhood Obesity Foundation.* Childhood Obesity Foundation, n.d. Web. 7 Aug. 2013.

CHAPTER 6. HEALTHY EATING FOR A HEALTHIER YOU

1. Sharon Palmer. "Shaping Up the Dietary Supplement Industry." *Today's Dietician* 9.1 (Jan. 2007). Web. 7 Aug. 2013.

2. John Hoffman, Judith A. Salerno, and Alexandra Moss. *The Weight of the Nation: To Win We Have to Lose*. New York: St. Martin's, 2012. Print. 57.

3. Debasis Bagchi and Harry G. Preuss, eds. *Obesity: Epidemiology, Pathophysiology, and Prevention*. New York: CRC, 2013. Print. 920.

4. John Hoffman, Judith A. Salerno, and Alexandra Moss. *The Weight of the Nation: To Win We Have to Lose*. New York: St. Martin's, 2012. Print. 92.

5. Ibid. 49.

6. Adam Drewnowski and S. E. Specter. "Poverty and Obesity." *American Journal of Clinical Nutrition* 79 (2004): 10. Print.

7. Ibid. 7.

CHAPTER 7. MAKING TIME TO MOVE

1. "'Biggest Loser': Where Are They Now?" *Today Reality TV*. Today.com, n.d. Web. 7 Aug. 2013.

2. Yoni Freedhoff. "The Real Biggest Losers? The Show's Audience." Huffpost Living. *Huffington Post*. 14 Jan. 2013. Web. 7 Aug. 2013.

3. Ibid.

4. John Hoffman, Judith A. Salerno, and Alexandra Moss. *The Weight of the Nation: To Win We Have to Lose*. New York: St. Martin's, 2012. Print. 170.

CHAPTER 8. BEYOND DIET AND EXERCISE

1. Debasis Bagchi and Harry G. Preuss, eds. *Obesity: Epidemiology, Pathophysiology, and Prevention*. New York: CRC, 2013. Print. 315.

2. "Obesity: Treatment and Drugs." *Mayo Clinic*. Mayo Foundation, 7 June 2013. Web. 7 Aug. 2013.

3. D. Kendall, et al. "Metformin in Obese Children and Adolescents." *Journal of Clinical Endocrinology and Metabolism* 98.1 (2013): 325. Print.

4. Raquel Maurier. "New Gene Therapy Approach Could Improve Obesity Treatment." *University of Alberta News*. University of Alberta, 19 Sep. 2012. Web. 7 Aug. 2013.

5. Debasis Bagchi and Harry G. Preuss, eds. *Obesity: Epidemiology, Pathophysiology, and Prevention*. New York: CRC, 2013. Print. 956.

6. "Obesity: Treatment and Drugs." *Mayo Clinic*. Mayo Foundation, 7 June 2013. Web. 7 Aug. 2013.

7. Terrence E. Steyer and Adrienne Ables. "Complementary and Alternative Therapies for Weight Loss." *Primary Care: Clinics in Office Practice* 36 (2009): 395. Print.

CHAPTER 9. COPING AND SUPPORT

1. Jonah Lehrer. "Don't! The Secret of Self-Control." *New Yorker*. New Yorker, 18 May 2009. Web. 7 Aug. 2013.

2. John Hoffman, Judith A. Salerno, and Alexandra Moss. *The Weight of the Nation: To Win We Have to Lose*. New York: St. Martin's, 2012. Print. 113.

3. Ibid. 142.

INDEX

ABOUT THE AUTHOR

L. E. Carmichael never outgrew that stage of childhood when nothing's more fun than amazing your friends with your stockpile of weird and wonderful facts. Her sense of wonder came in handy during her career as a scientist, and in 2006, she received the Governor General's Medal for her PhD thesis, Ecological Genetics of Northern Wolves and Arctic Foxes. She's written about everything from animal migration to hybrid cars, and her most recent children's science book is *Fox Talk: How Some Very Special Animals Helped Scientists Understand Communication.*